Taking Your Camera to ARGENTINA

Ted Park

Raintree Steck-Vaughn Publishers
A Harcourt Company

Austin · New York
www.steck-vaughn.com

Copyright © 2001, Steck-Vaughn Company

All rights reserved. No part of this book may be reproduced or utilized in any form or by any means, electronic or mechanical, including photocopying, recording, or by any information storage and retrieval system, without permission in writing from the publisher. Inquiries should be addressed to copyright permissions, Steck-Vaughn Company, P.O. Box 26015, Austin, TX 78755.

Published by Raintree Steck-Vaughn Publishers,
an imprint of Steck-Vaughn Company

Library of Congress Cataloging-in-Publication Data is available upon request

Printed in the United States of America
10 9 8 7 6 5 4 3 2 1 W 03 02 01 00

Cover photo: Lavalle Monument & Plaza in Buenos Aires

Title page photo: Bas Relief, La Boca, The Caminito in Buenos Aires

Photo acknowledgments

Contents

You're in Argentina!	4
Looking at the Land	6
Buenos Aires	10
Great Places to Visit	12
The People	14
How Do People Live in Argentina?	16
Government and Religion	18
Earning a Living	20
School and Sports	22
Food and Holiday Fun	24
The Future	26
Quick Facts About Argentina	28
Glossary	30
Index	32

# You're in Argentina!

Argentina is the second largest country in South America. Brazil is the only country that is larger.

Argentina's land changes a great deal from the north to the south end of the country. There are tall mountains, volcanoes, tropical rain forests and plains. The largest desert in South America is located here, too.

Argentina has a few large cities. **Buenos Aires** is the largest city and it is also the capital. **Córdoba** and

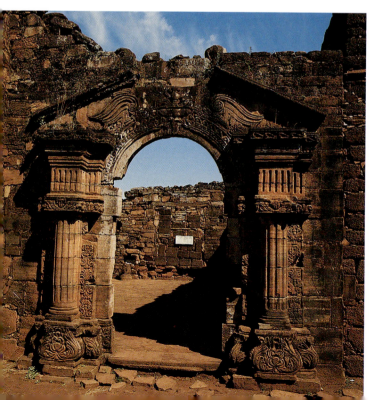

The San Ignacio Miní ruins in Misiones date back to the 17th and 18th centuries. Misiones is in the north of Argentina and borders Paraguay on the west.

This is the famous Cerro Torre in Patagonia. If you went from Misiones to Patagonia, you would pass through many different types of land.

Rosario are also major cities in Argentina.

The name Argentina comes from the Latin word *argentum*. This means silver. The country was named by Spanish explorers who went there to find great riches. Today, Spanish is the official language of Argentina.

This book will show you some of the best things to see in Argentina. You will learn interesting things about the country and the people who live there. So, when you're ready to take your camera there, you'll know exactly what to do and where to go. Enjoy your trip!

Looking at the Land

Argentina is about 2,300 miles (3,700 km) long from north to south and is approximately 980 miles (1,577 km) from east to west at its widest point. Argentina is 1,068,298 square miles (2,766,890 sq km). It is the eighth largest country in the world.

The country has a coastline along the south Atlantic Ocean that stretches for 3099 miles (4989 km). It shares a border with Chile to the west. The Andes Mountains run down this border. Bolivia and Paraguay are to the north, and Brazil and Uruguay to the northeast.

Argentina has the tallest mountain in the Western Hemisphere. It is called **Mount Aconcagua** and it is 22,831 feet (6,959 m) tall. Mount Aconcagua is part of the Andes mountains.

Many Different Kinds of Land

There are four main regions in Argentina: Mesopotamia, the **Gran Chaco**, the **Pampa** and

What do you like most, mountains, glaciers, lakes or woods? Rio Negro in Patagonia has everything!

Patagonia. Mesopotamia is the northeastern part of Argentina between the Paraná and the Uruguay rivers. Mesopotamia means *between the rivers* in the Greek language. There are more than 2,000 kinds of plants and 400 kinds of birds in this area.

The Gran Chaco is made up of wet plains where the grass can grow up to 8 feet (2.4 m) tall. In other areas, the Gran Chaco is dry with trees and bushes that are covered with thorns.

The Pampa is in central Argentina. Part of the Pampa is fertile, wet land that is good for farming.

The largest part of the Pampa is sandy and dry.

Patagonia is the largest region of Argentina. It is also the farthest south and has the largest desert in South America. Southern Patagonia has rocky cliffs, canyons and very few trees. The winters are very cold there. Northern Patagonia has sandy grasslands and irrigated farming.

The largest colony of Magellan penguins in the world is not in the South Pole. It's here in Punta Tombo, Patagonia.

Buenos Aires

The Largest City

Buenos Aires is Argentina's largest city and the nation's capital. It lies in eastern Argentina, along a bay called the Rio de la Plata. More than 12 million people live there. Most people live in barrios. Barrios are neighborhoods. Each barrio has its own churches, schools, and stores.

The Rio de la Plata is the border between Argentina and the country of Uruguay. The city is more than 400 years old.

Buenos Aires is a modern city, with large streets and boulevards. Did you know that the world's largest street is here? The Avenida 9 de Julio is 425 feet (130 m) wide. The National Museum of Fine Arts, the National Historical Museum, and the National Library are all here. Make sure you get a snapshot of the Colón Theater too.

The Colón Theater is one of the world's famous opera houses. It is beautiful, isn't it? This is a great place to take your camera.

# Great Places to Visit

Tierra del Fuego is at the southern tip of Argentina. Argentina and Chile share Tierra del Fuego. The name Tierra del Fuego is Spanish for *land of fire*. The town of Ushuaia is located there and has a population of about 14,000 people.

Iguazú Falls

The Iguazú waterfalls are located at the Argentina-Brazil border. **Iguazú Falls** looks like a stretched-out

The town of Ushuaia in Tierra Del Fuego is the world's most southern port. It's only 650 miles (1,046 km) from the South Pole.

If you go to Misiones, you should not miss the Iguazú Falls. You will be able to see many rainbows by the Argentina-Brazil border.

horseshoe. The falls run for 1.7 miles (2.7 km). Several islands on the edge of the falls divide the river into some 275 separate waterfalls. The water falls between 200 and 269 feet (60 and 82 m) to the river below. The water falling causes a rainbow mist that rises about 500 feet (150 m) into the air. The area is so beautiful that it has been set aside as a national park.

The People

Europeans in South America

The first European settlers came from Spain, Italy, and Portugal in the early 1500s. Others came from Great Britain, Germany, France, and other European countries. Italians make up the largest group of Argentineans with a common ancestry. Ancestry means the ancestors or members of a family who lived

These university students from Mendoza are taking a break from studying. Most Argentineans finish high school and many go on to college.

In the 18th century, you could find gauchos or cowboys living on the Pampa. Today, the gaucho takes care of sheep and other animals on large ranches.

a long time ago. Today more people come from the Middle East and Asia. There are so many different types of people. Read about the **gaucho** in the picture above.

However, less than three percent of the population living in Argentina today are Amerindian or native to the area. Most of the three percent are **mestizos**, people with Amerindian and European ancestors.

How Do People Live in Argentina?

Most Argentineans live in cities where there are more ways to earn a living. Women make up a large portion of the workforce in Argentina. Many of them are doctors, lawyers, and educators. In cities, people can live in apartment buildings, mansions or bungalows with small yards. A bungalow is a small house. In the country, poor people may have adobe homes with dirt floors. Rich people's homes are generally built surrounding a courtyard. A courtyard is an area surrounded by walls. These homes are built on *estancias*. This is Spanish for large farms.

A very small part of the Argentine population lives in the countryside. Most live in cities because of the need to earn a living.

Argentina has a middle class too. Middle class means the part of the population that is not rich but not poor. The middle class makes up a large part of the

There are many businesswomen in Argentina who have important jobs. It is easier for them to find work in larger cities, like this one.

population. In other countries in South America, the people are usually very poor or very rich.

The Tango

A dance called the **tango** comes from Argentina. The tango is the national dance of Argentina. The dance is said to show the happiness and sadness of life.

Government and Religion

Government

Argentina is a federal republic made up of 22 **provinces**, Tierra del Fuego, and the federal district of Buenos Aires. Provinces are like states. Argentina is a **democracy** similar to the United States. The National Congress makes the laws. The National Congress is made up of the Senate and the Chamber of Deputies.

People in Argentina over 18 must vote in elections.

The people elect the president for four years. The president and vice president of Argentina must be Catholic.

Religion

Almost all Argentineans are Roman Catholic. There are a few Protestants, and about 400,000 Jewish people live in the city of Buenos Aires.

America has a White House, and Argentina has a Pink House! The Casa Rosada (Pink House) is where the President of Argentina lives. It is on the world's widest street, Avenida 9 de Julio.

Earning a Living

Although Argentina is one of the most modern of South American countries, farming still exists. Wheat, corn, and other grains are major crops. The rich soil of the Pampa is good for farming. Fruit from orchards and vineyards is exported around the world. Exports are goods that are taken out of a country and sold for

These boats bring in lots of fish into the port at Mar del Plata every day. If you don't like beef, you can eat fish instead.

Cattle driving in Corrientes. Here is where modern gauchos work.

profit. Beef is an important export for Argentina. Argentina's beef is sent all around the world.

Where the land is not good enough for farming, it is often good for raising and feeding sheep and other animals. Sheep provide wool. This is another major source of income for Argentineans.

Fishing is a large business too. Fishermen bring in huge catches of sardines, anchovies, and tuna.

School and Sports

School

From the ages of 6 to 14, Argentine children must go to school. At the age of 14, many children go to high school. More than half a million Argentineans go to college each year.

Sports

Soccer is the most popular sport in Argentina. Argentine soccer teams are among the best in the world and often play in the World Cup. Argentineans also love horses and enjoy horseback riding. This comes from the gauchos who rode horses on the Pampa. **Pato** is a popular sport in Argentina. Pato is the Spanish word for duck. Players on horseback grasp the duck or ball by leather thongs and try to throw it into a goal fitted with nets. They also enjoy tennis, basketball, and rugby. Auto racing and boxing are also well liked in Argentina.

This is a soccer team in Buenos Aires. Children begin playing soccer at a very young age. When they grow up, if they don't become professional players, they become really big fans!

Argentineans love horses and polo is a very important sport there. They have a world-class reputation in polo.

Food and Holiday Fun

Let's Eat!

Food is plentiful in Argentina. Beef is very popular because there is so much of it. Argentineans love barbecues which are called *asado* in Spanish. Special meat dishes include **empañadas** and locro. Empañadas are small pies filled with beef, vegetables, or cheese. Locro is a thick stew with beef, sausage, corn, beans, and other vegetables.

A popular drink in Argentina is called **yerba maté**. It is a drink like tea. It is made from a grass that grows in the Pampa. Traditionally, people sip it through a silver straw (called bombilla) from a special kind of cup.

Celebrate!

Many holidays in Argentina are those of the Roman Catholic Church. Both Easter and Christmas are well-known holidays. **Carnaval** (which is spelled carnival in English) celebrations happen on the day before Lent

These Argentineans are relaxing and watching the city go by. In Argentina, it's very common to see people drinking maté while relaxing on a park bench, or sitting and talking with friends.

begins. During Carnaval, people parade, dance, and have a good time. May 25th is the anniversary of the 1810 revolution, when Argentina fought against Spanish control of Argentina.

The Future

If you took your camera to Argentina, you would see a large and exciting country. There is a lot of poverty in Argentina even though there is a large middle class. People in the government are working to get rid of poverty. The Argentineans are trying to make sure that everyone has decent health care and a good education.

Argentina has gone through some difficult times with high unemployment and high prices. Unemployment in a country means the number of people who cannot find a job. The economy now seems to be improving and people are working and able to afford what they need and want.

Argentina has some problems with pollution. The biggest problem areas are near Buenos Aires and other large cities. Argentina has set up national parks to save some of the beautiful countryside from development. National parks provide places where animals can live safely as well.

Buenos Aires is a modern city of the future mixed with old-world charm. When you go, you will be able to take lots of pictures of buildings like this. Enjoy your trip!

When you leave Argentina, someone may say **¡Adiós!** (ah-dee-OS) This is the Spanish word for good-bye.

Quick Facts About ARGENTINA

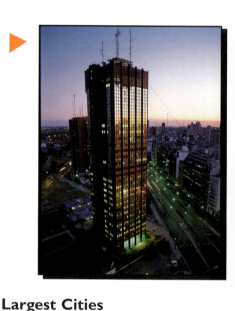

Capital
Buenos Aires

Borders
Chile, Bolivia, Paraguay, Brazil, Uruguay

Area
1,068,298 square miles
(2,766,890 sq km)

Population
36,955,182

Largest Cities
Buenos Aires (12,960,976); Córdoba (1,148,345); Rosario (894,645)

Chief crops
grains, corn, sugar, beets, sorghum, soybeans

Natural resources
fertile plains of the Pampa, lead, zinc, copper, tin, uranium, iron ore, petroleum

Longest river
Paraná: 3,032 miles (4,880 km)

Flag of Argentina

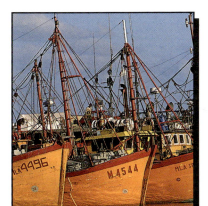

▶ **Coastline**
2,140 miles (3,444 km)

Monetary unit
nuevo Peso Argentino (peso)

Literacy rate
96 percent of Argentineans can read and write.

Major industries
food processing, automobiles, steel, textiles, chemicals, printing

Glossary

Buenos Aires: (BWEN-ohs Ahr-es) The capital of Argentina, and its largest city.

Carnaval: (Kar-nuh-vuhl) A celebration that is held in many Roman Catholic countries just before the start of Lent.

Córdoba: (KOR-doh-bah) Argentina's second largest city, a metalworking center, and a popular resort.

democracy: (di-MOK-ruh-see) A way of governing in which the people choose leaders in elections.

empañadas: (em-pahn-YA-dahs) Small pies filled with beef, vegetables, or cheese.

gauchos: (gow-chose) The cowboys that live in Argentina's Pampa.

Gran Chaco: (grahn choco) A dry part of Argentina known for its animal life, grasslands, and thorny forests.

Iguazú Falls: (i-gwah-SU fawls) A waterfall on the border of Brazil and Argentina.

mestizos: (meh-STEE-sos) People of mixed Amerindian and European blood.

Mount Aconcagua: (ah-cone-cah-gwah) The tallest

mountain in the Western Hemisphere.

Pampa: (PAHM-pah) A fertile flat region in central Argentina where most Argentineans live.

Patagonia: (PAH-tah-GO-nee-ah) A harsh, dry, flat area in southern Argentina between the Andes and the Atlantic Ocean.

pato: (PAH-toh) A sport in which players on horseback grab the pato or ball by leather thongs and throw it into a goal.

province: (PROV-unhss) An area of a country similar to a state in the U.S.

Rosario: (roh-SAH-ree-oh) A river port on the Paraná River and the third largest city in Argentina.

tango: (TANG-oh) An Argentinean dance that expresses the passion and sadness of life.

Tierra del Fuego: (tee-EH-rrah dehl FWEH-go) A group of islands at the southern tip of Argentina. Tierra del Fuego means Land of Fire.

yerba maté: (YEHR-bah ma-TEH) A popular Argentinean drink made from a grass that grows in the Pampa.

Index

Amerindians 15
Andes Mountains 6
asado 24

bombilla 24
Buenos Aires 4, 10, 18

Chile 6, 12
Córdoba 4

empañadas 24
estancia 16

gaucho 15
Gran Chaco 6, 8,

Iguazú Falls 12, 13

Mesopotamia 6, 8
mestizo 15
Mount Aconcagua 6

National Congress 18
national parks 13, 27

Pampa 6, 8, 9, 20
Paraná River 8
Patagonia 8, 9
pato 22
pollution 26

religion 18
Rio de la Plata 10
Rosario 5

settlers 14
soccer 22
Spanish: explorers 5; language 5

tango 17
Tierra del Fuego 12

Ushuaia 12

yerba maté 24

ABB-3460

982 Par

Park, Ted, 1969-
A30229011536546B
Taking your camera to
Argentina /
c2001.